Starting out in
Maths

Book 1

Ann Douglas, Valerie Ellis and Jim Boucher

for 7-8 year olds

Letts

My grandfather is very busy. He mends clocks and watches. Please make each clock show the correct time.

5.30 p.m.

8 o'clock

Four-thirty

Quarter past 2

9 : 45

3 o'clock

Half past 7

Quarter to ten

Tie the correct tag on each clock.

Ten-thirty

3.15

Six o'clock

Quarter past 8

Half past seven

Quarter to 11

2 o'clock

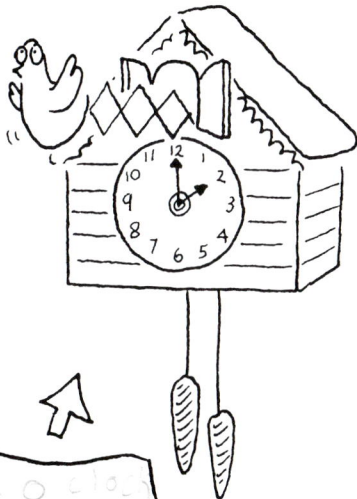

2 o'clock

3·15

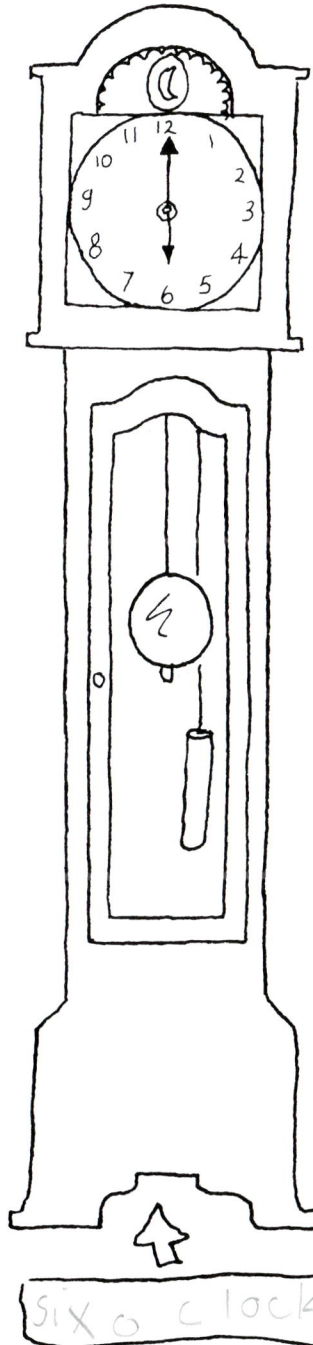

ten-thirty

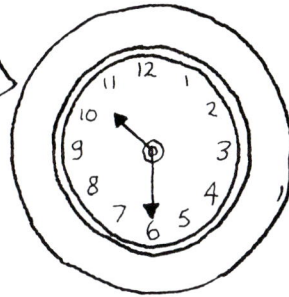

Quarter to 11

8:15

Quarter past 8

Half past seven

Six o'clock

▶ Now colour in the clocks.

3

Look at how the numbers are formed in the display window of your calculator.

I have coloured in this grid to form the number seven.

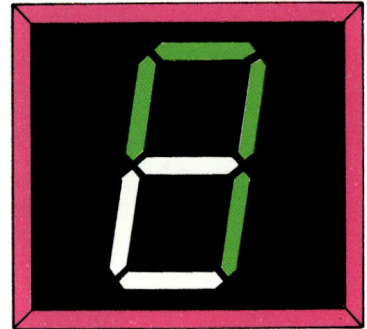

▶ Colour in these grids to form the numbers 0, 1, 2, 3, 4, 5, 6, 7, 8 and 9 as they show in a calculator display window.

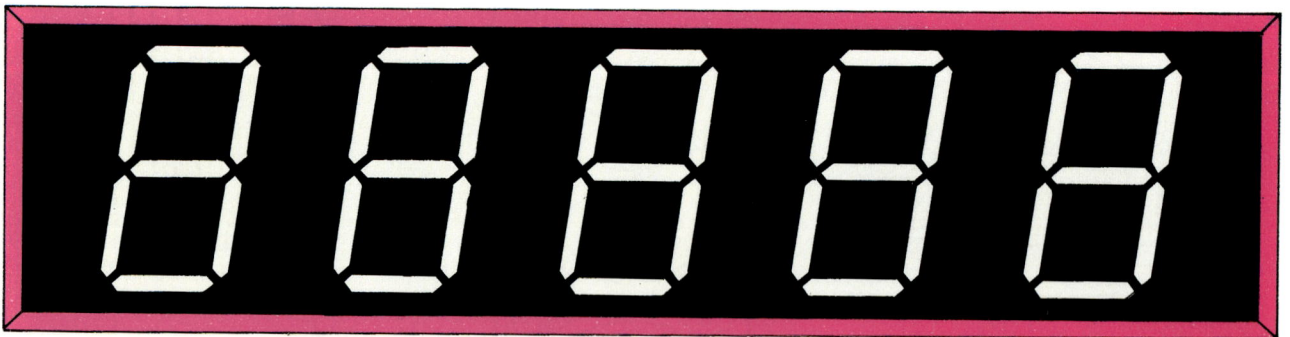

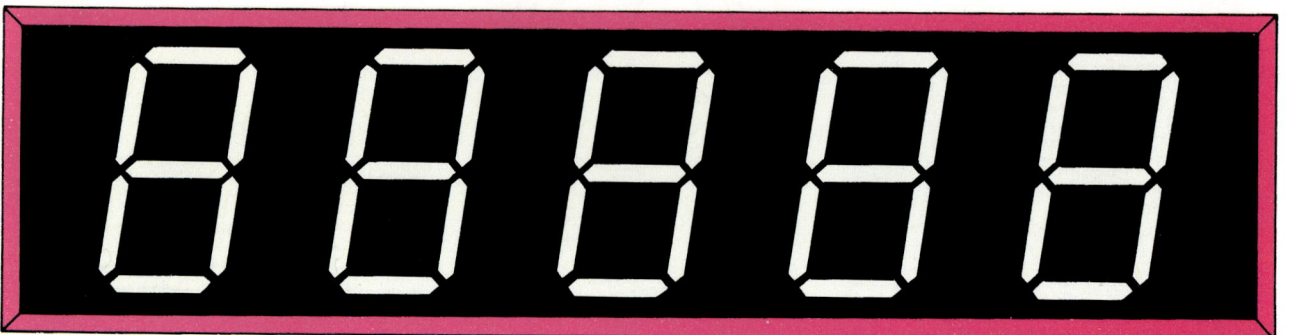

▶ Look at this section of number keys on your calculator.

Let's look for patterns.

▶ Add the diagonals.

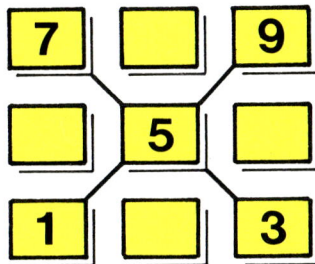

$7 + 5 + 3 =$ _____
$1 + 5 + 9 =$ _____

▶ Add the middle row, then add the middle column.

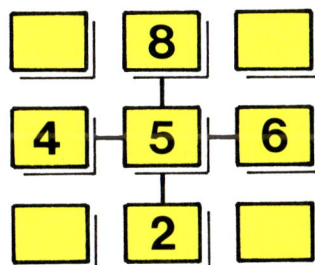

$4 + 5 + 6 =$ _____
$8 + 5 + 2 =$ _____

The patterns in these last two sets are harder to spot.

▶ Now add the rows.

$7 + 8 + 9 =$ _____
$4 + 5 + 6 =$ _____
$1 + 2 + 3 =$ _____

▶ Finally, add the columns.

$7 + 4 + 1 =$ _____
$8 + 5 + 2 =$ _____
$9 + 6 + 3 =$ _____

▶ Give yourself a big 'HOORAY' if you spotted them.

5

3 Shapes in shops

Just like us, shapes have faces which help us to recognize them. I like to sort out the different shapes when I am in the supermarket.

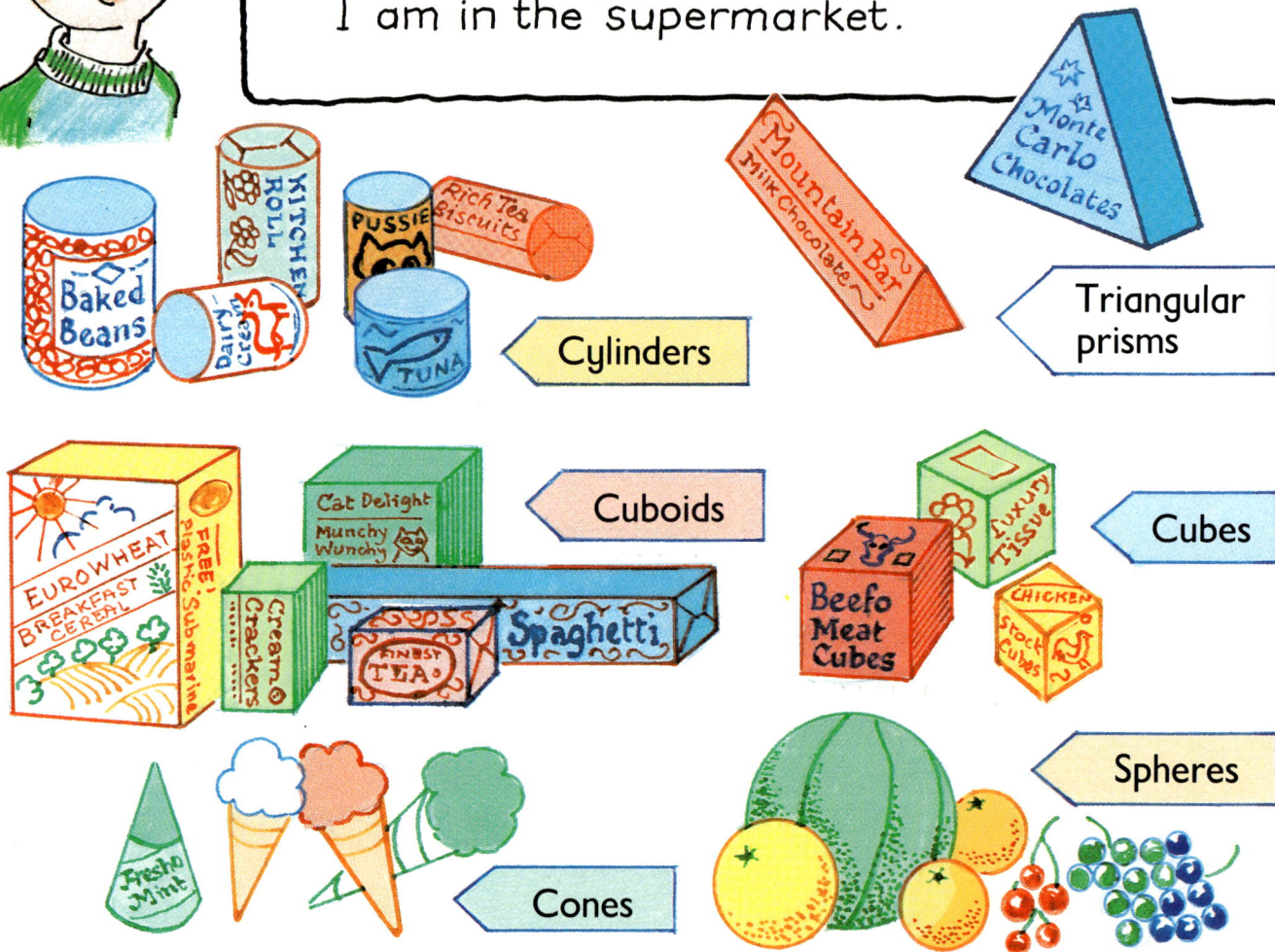

Cylinders

Triangular prisms

Cuboids

Cubes

Cones

Spheres

▶ Make a list of the shapes you have seen.

Cylinders	Cubes	Cuboids	Cones	Spheres
Cat Food	Tissues			

▶ Colour in each face that you need to make the shape.
If you draw a smiley face first, it might help.

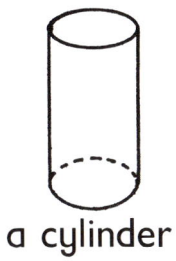

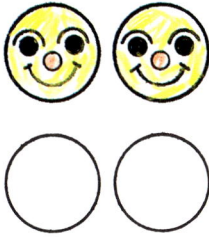

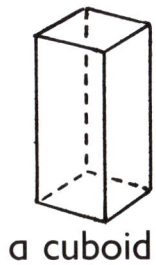

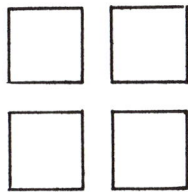

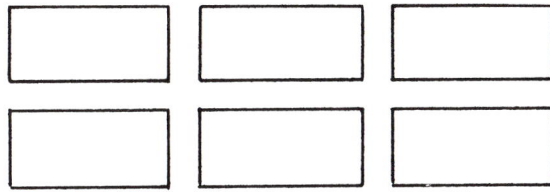

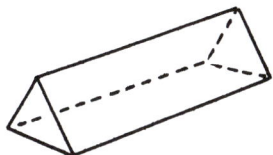

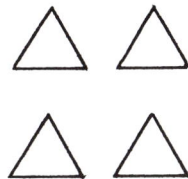

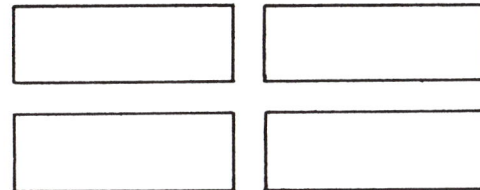

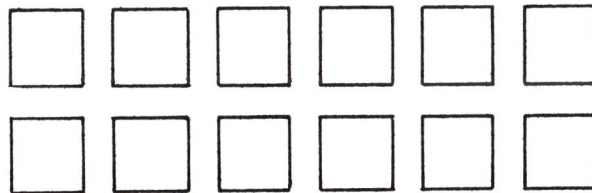

a cylinder

a cuboid

a triangular prism

a cube

▶ Fill in the chart to show which plane shapes
made the solid shapes.

SHAPE	circles	rectangles	squares	triangles
cylinder	2	1	○	○
cuboid				
triangular prism				
cube				

4 Number tracking

Here are some sections of number tracks.
Some of the numbers are missing.

▶ Fill in the missing numbers.

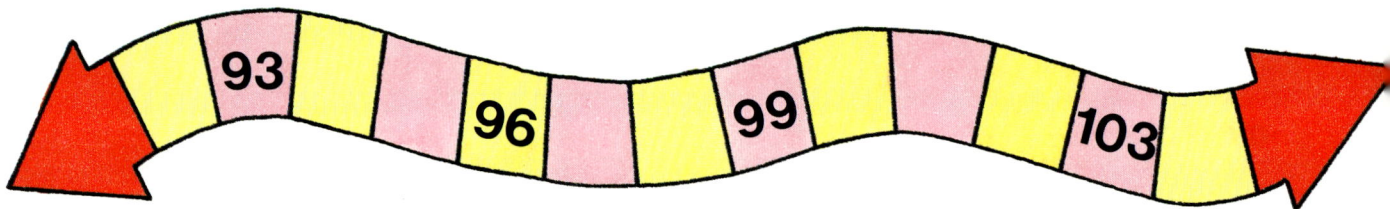

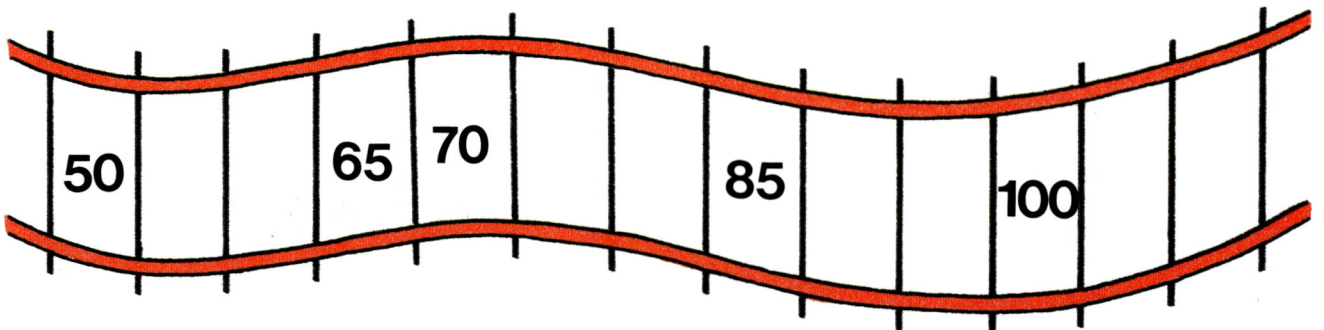

43 · 45 · 47 · · · 51 · · · 55 ·

93 · 96 · · 99 · · 103 ·

50 · 70 · · 100 · 120 · ·

26 · 28 · · · 34 · ·

50 · · 65 · 70 · · · 85 · · · 100

21 · 23 · · · 31 · · 35 · · · 43

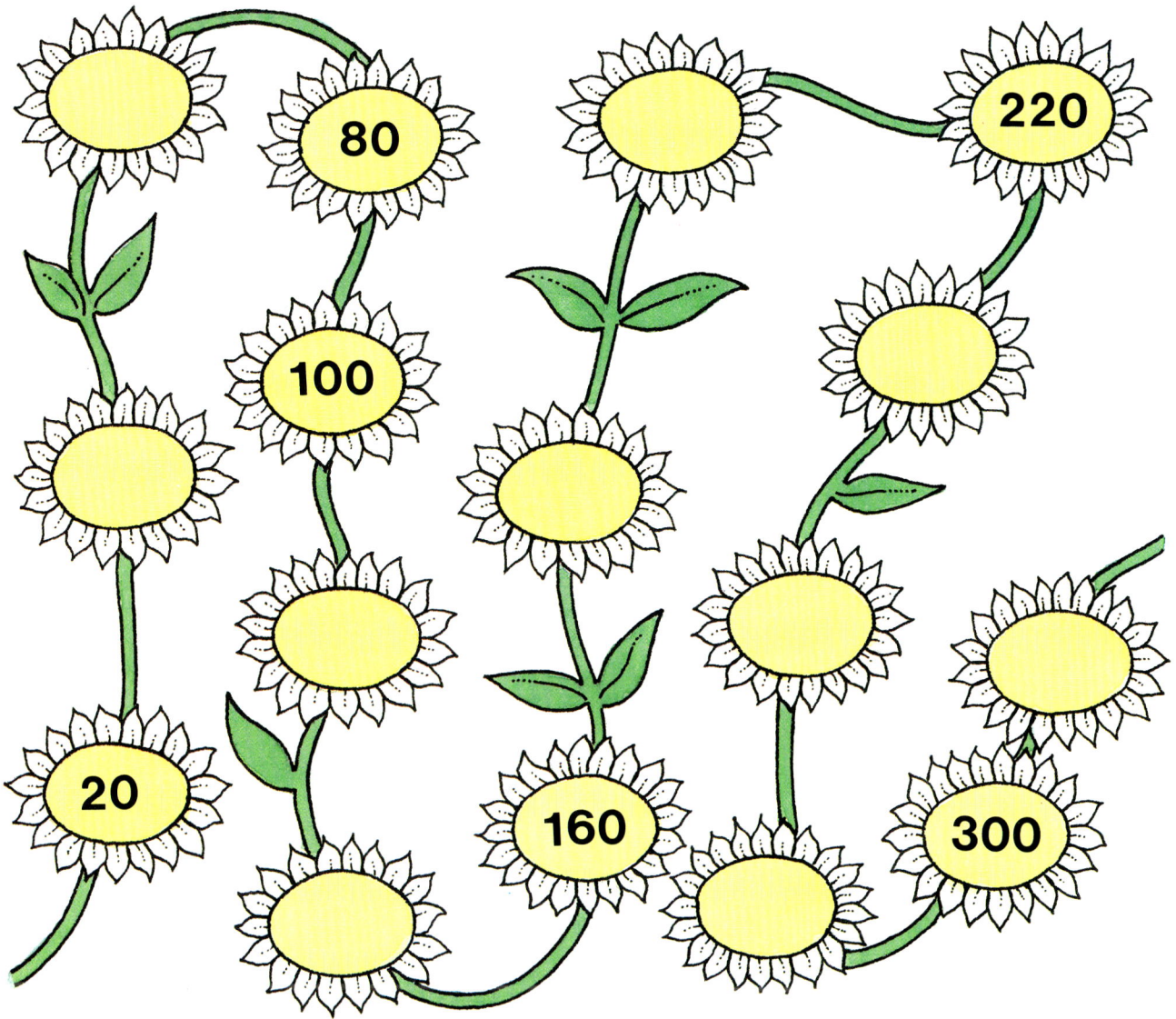

80

220

100

20

160

300

▶ Mark the following numbers on the number line below.

The first two have been done for you.

19   43   35   45

27   16   48   24

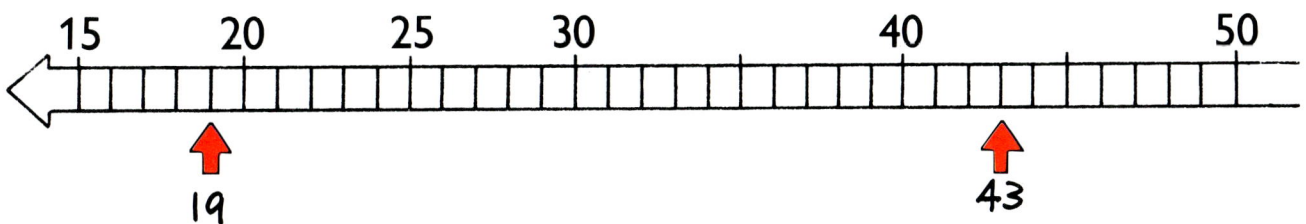

15   20   25   30   40   50

19

43

5 | Body measures

Make your own personal measures from strips of paper. It is fun to guess first and then check with your own ruler. You will need paper, pencil and scissors.

Take care with the scissors!

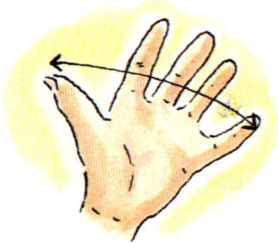

hand-span

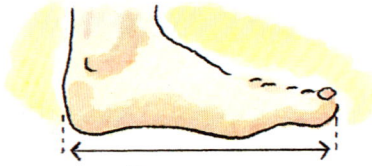

footstep

cubit

reach

stride

Just take a big step.
Don't do the splits!

Find your own height using your personal measures.
Then find the length, width and height of five more things. I've given you three ideas to start with.

Here is a chart for you to fill in. If you make another one for a grown-up you may be able to talk about the differences you find.

▶ Write down what you measured.

	How many?				
	spans	cubits	reaches	strides	footsteps
My height					
Table — length					
Table — width					
Table — height					
Bed — length					
Bed — width					
Bed — height					
Bath — length					
Bath — width					
Bath — height					
length					
width					
height					
length					
width					
height					

What do you think a grown-up's chart would look like?

More or less in between

▶ Squeeze a number between each pair of numbers below.

(34) (?) (39) ➡ (34) (36) (39)

35, 37 or 38 would also be correct.

(19) ( ) (23)

(54) ( ) (45)

(93) ( ) (101)

(112) ( ) (108)

(485) ( ) (308)

(900) ( ) (1000)

▶ Draw a ring around the **larger** number in each pair.

| 52, 25 | 13, 31 | 112, 121 | 101, 110 |

▶ Draw a ring around the **smallest** number in each group.

| 21, 19, 43 | 210, 121, 102 | 166, 213, 191 | 340, 403, 304 |

Gary and Tammy had four sets of cards, numbered from 0 to 9.
They shuffled the cards and placed them face down
in the centre of the table.

Gary went first.
He had to call

'Highest' or 'Lowest'.

HIGHEST

Tammy dealt two cards each.
They looked at their cards.

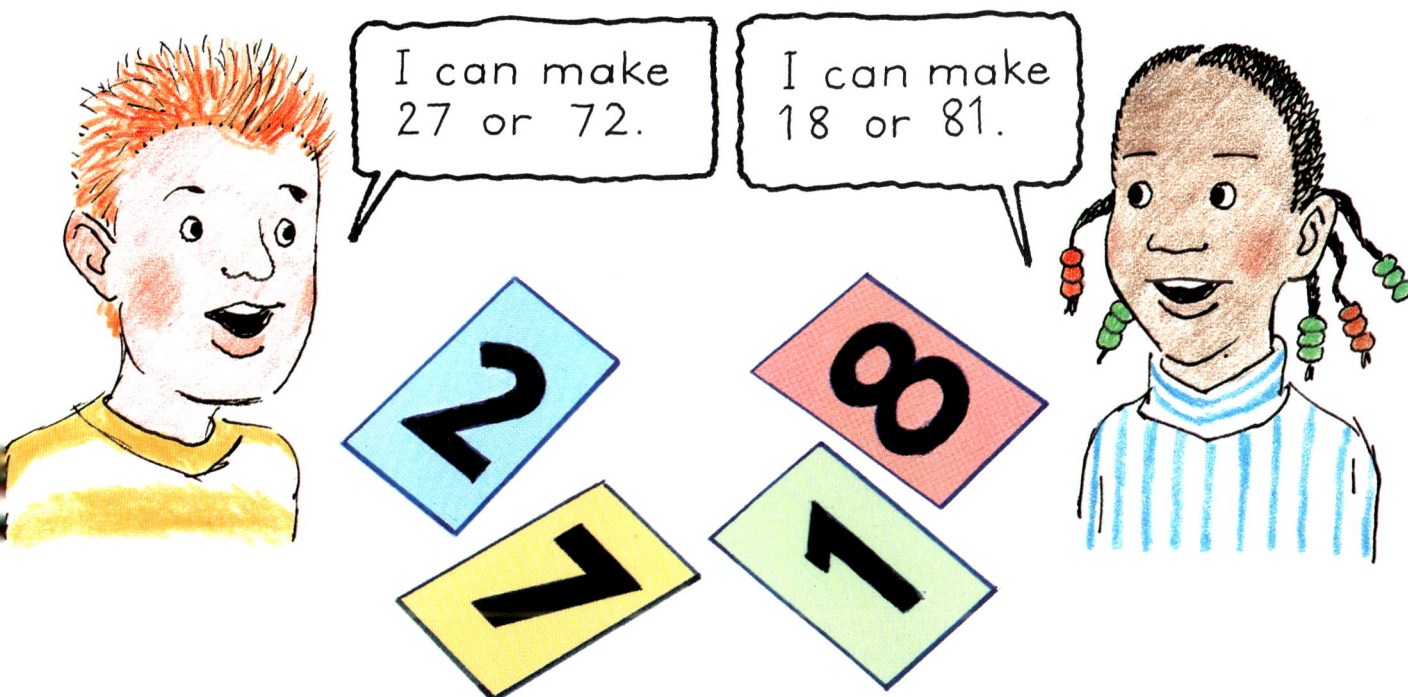

I can make
27 or 72.

I can make
18 or 81.

Tammy could make the
highest number......81
so she scored 1 point.

▶ Play this game with a friend or relative.

▶ Take turns to call 'Highest' or 'Lowest'.

▶ Try playing the game, dealing 3 cards each.

1 Bulk buying

> Many things can be bought in packs of ten. Here are just a few.

Crisps

Bags of 10 packets   Single packets

▶ How many bags of 10 packets _____ and how many single packets _____?

▶ How many packets of crisps altogether _____?

Eggs

Boxes of 10 eggs   Single eggs

▶ How many boxes of 10 eggs _____ and how many single eggs _____?

▶ How many eggs altogether _____?

If you can count in tens then you can add very quickly.

▶ Fill in the spaces below.

Salt and Vinegar

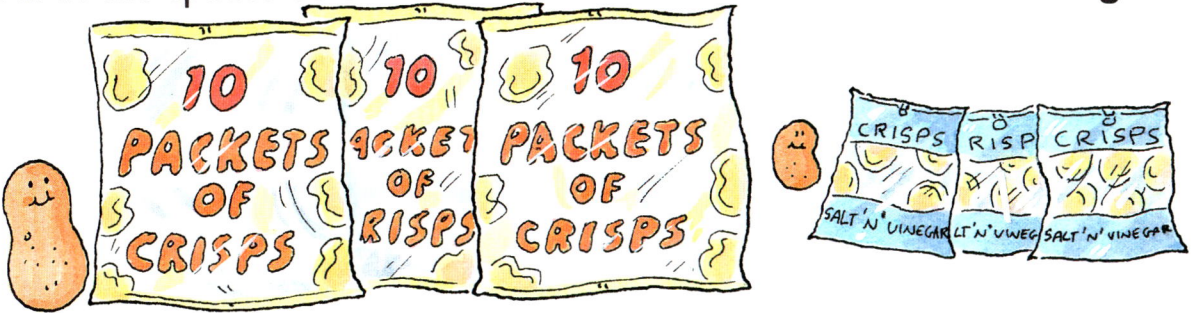

There are _____ bags and _____ packets of salt and vinegar crisps.

Cheese and Onion

There are _____ bags and _____ packets of cheese and onion crisps.

So, there are _____ packets of crisps altogether.

Brown Eggs

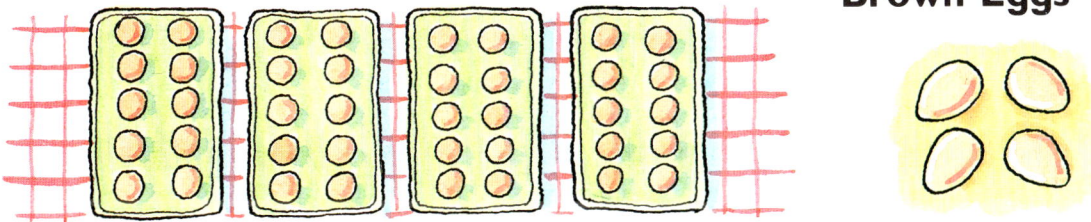

There are _____ boxes and _____ single brown eggs.

White Eggs

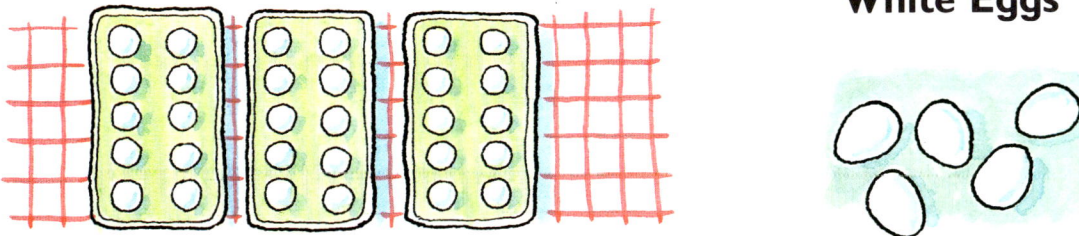

There are _____ boxes and _____ single white eggs.

So, there are _____ eggs altogether.

8 Double treble troubles

The numbers on the snake, from tail to head: 1, 2, 3, 4, 5, 6, 7, 8, 9, 10, 11, 12, 13, 14, 15, 16, 17, 18, 19, 20, 21, 22, 23, 24, 25, 26, 27, 28, 29, 30, 31, 32, 33, 34, 35, 36

▶ Count in 2s from the tail and put a ◯ round each number you land on.
Gary has done the first two for you.

▶ Now count in 3s from the tail and put a ✕ on each number you land on.
Gary has done the first two for you.

▶ Which numbers have both a ◯ and a ✕ ?

▶ Write them here: _____

► Put the correct number on each cherry.
Tom has done one for you.

You can use the snake to help you.

8 2×4   3×6   2×3   3×10

3×3   2×5   3×5   2×7

► Draw lines to show which flowers each butterfly can visit.
Ruth has done one for you.

2×6   3×4   2×12   3×2

3×5   12   15   24   6

3×6

18

2×10   20   8

2×9

3×8   2×3   2×4

9 Pocket money

Use coins to put the right money in each purse.

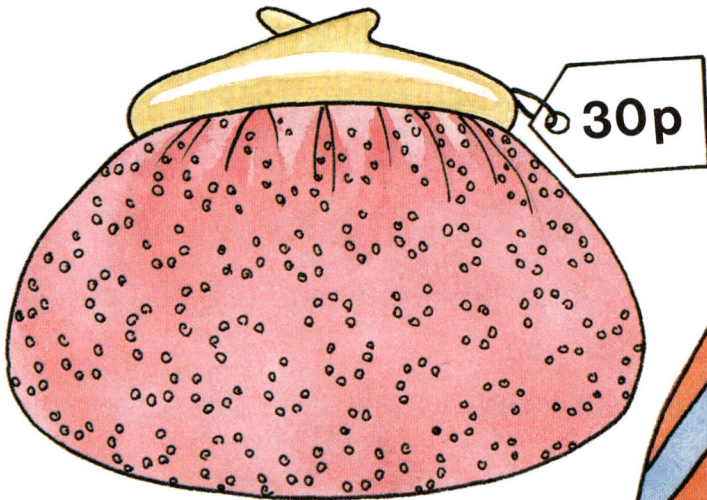

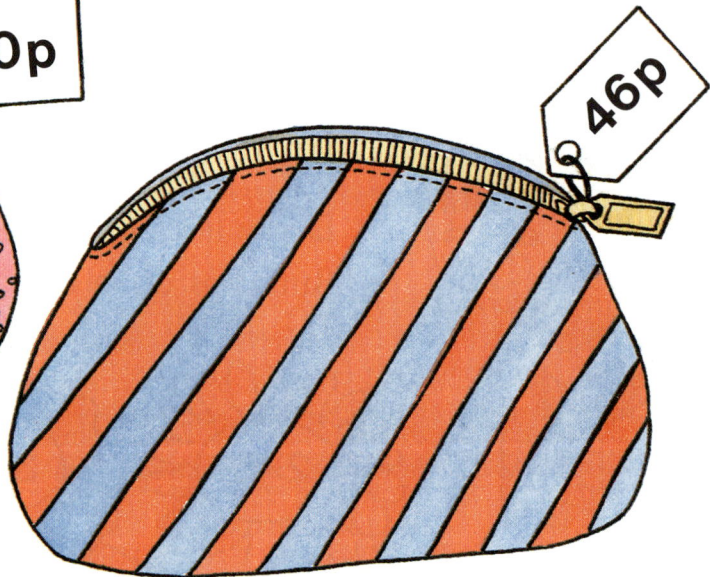

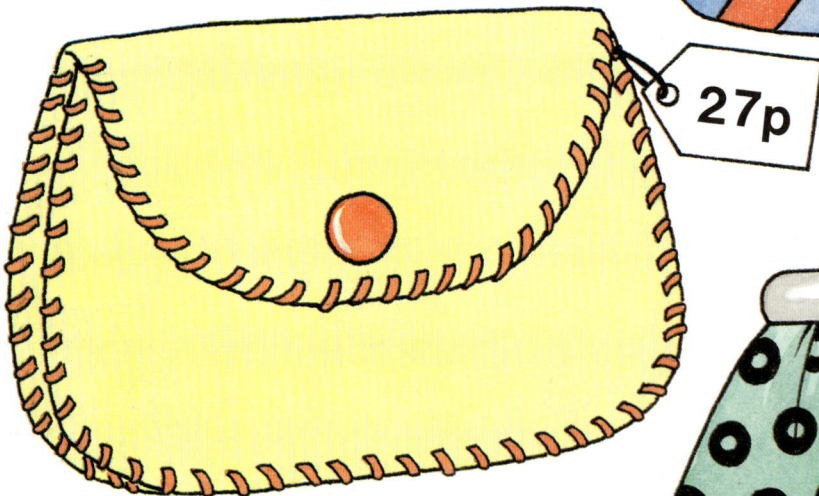

30p

46p

27p

£1·05

Add up the money in each purse.

1

2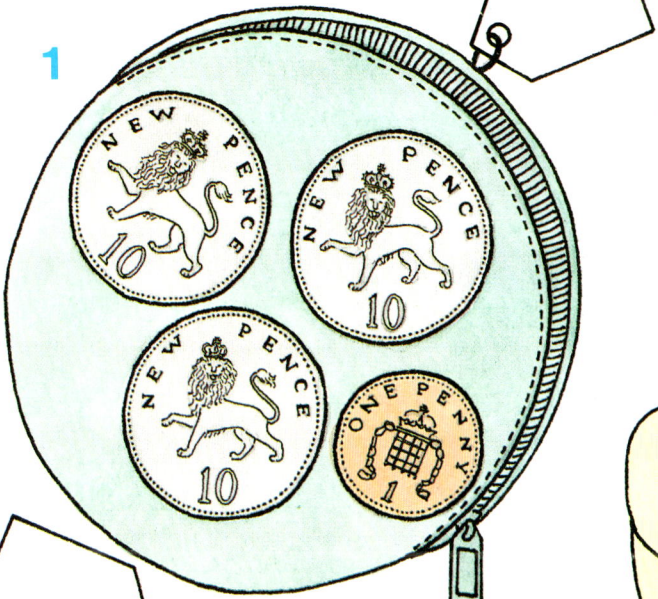

3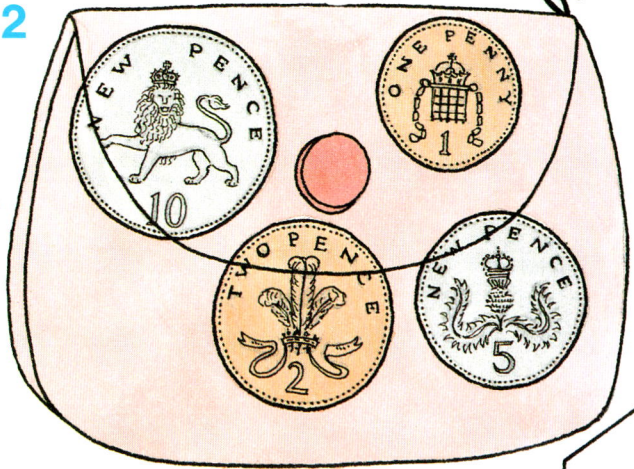

4

5

19

The chocolate box

Tony was given an ENORMOUS box of assorted chocolates.

This chart was on the back of the box.

⬤	Coffee Cream	🍬	Dairy Toffee
◆	Coconut	❤	Strawberry Cream
▭	Orange Cream	▣	Caramel
☁	Nut Cluster	🍬	Fudge
⬭	Chocolate Eclair	⬤	Brazil Nut in Chocolate

Tony counted the chocolates and started a tally chart.
▶ Can you finish it for him?

One → I
Two → II
Three → III
Four → IIII
Five → IIII

Kinds of chocolates	Tally	Total
Coffee Cream	IIII I	6
Dairy Toffee	IIII IIII I	
Coconut		4
Strawberry Cream	IIII	
Orange Cream	III	
Caramel		9
Nut Cluster	IIII III	
Fudge	II	
Chocolate Eclair		7
Brazil Nut in Chocolate	IIII	

▶ Complete this chart to show the kinds of
chocolates in Tony's box.
Give your chart a title.

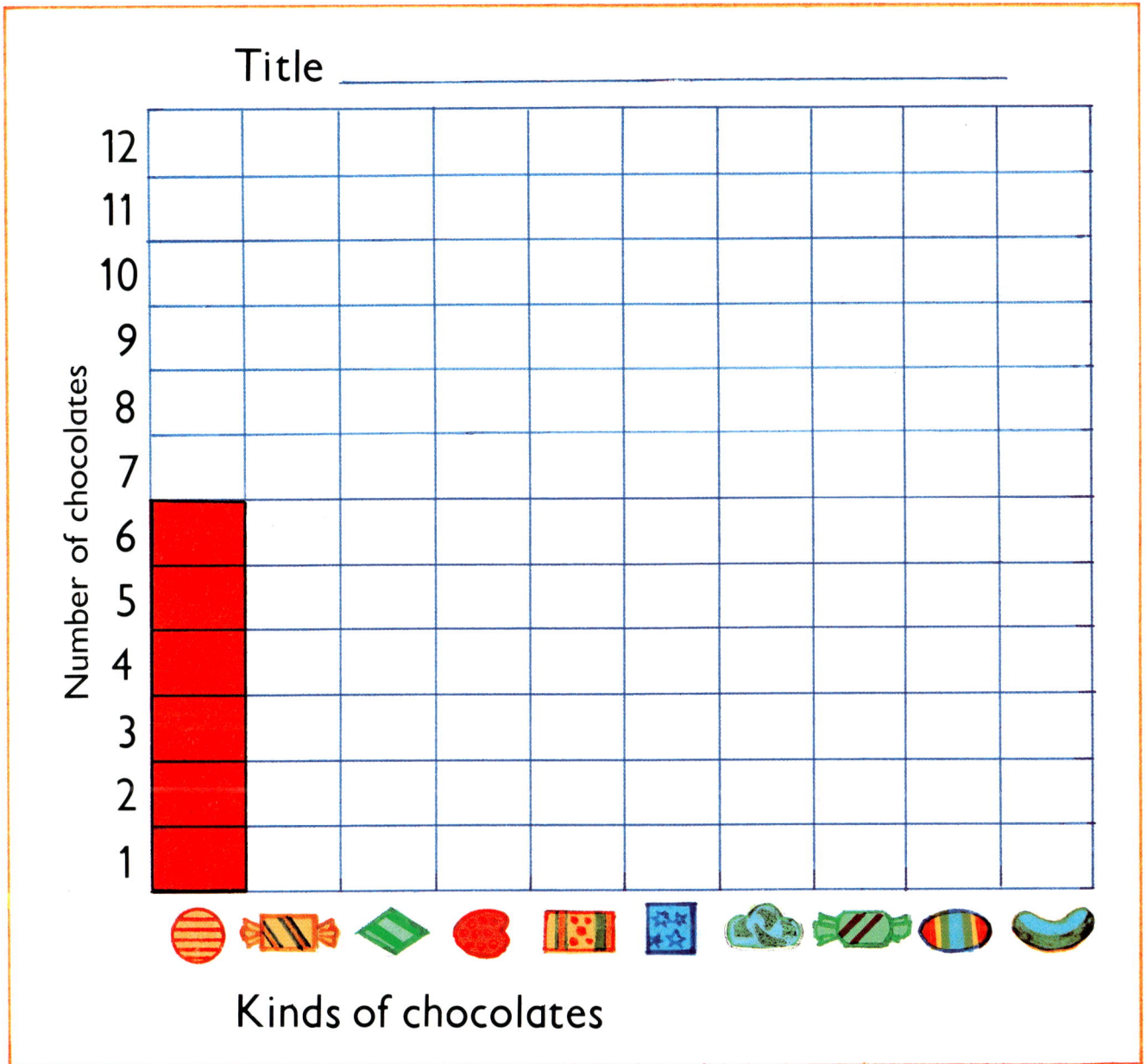

Title _____

Number of chocolates

12									
11									
10									
9									
8									
7									
6									
5									
4									
3									
2									
1									

Kinds of chocolates

1 How many more ⬜s were there than 🍬? _____

2 Which kind of chocolates were there most of? _____

3 Which kind of chocolates were there least of? _____

4 How many chocolates were in the box altogether? _____

Use coins to help you to answer these questions. Make sure you remove all the coins before starting the next question.

If you use 10p pieces you will need to change a 10p for ten 1p pieces before you can take away.

1 Put 23p in the

Take away 15p.

How much is left in the ? _____ p

2 Put 44p in the 🐷

Take away 28p.

How much is left in the 🐷 ?　　　———————P

3 Put 36p in the 🐷

Take away 17p.

How much is left in the 🐷 ?　　　———————P

4 Put 21p in the 🐷

Take away 13p.

How much is left in the 🐷 ?　　　———————P

5 Put 42p in the 🐷

Take away 27p.

How much is left in the 🐷 ?　　　———————P

I took 19p out
of the 🐷

There was still 13p
left in the 🐷

How much was in the 🐷
at the start ?

6 ————— P

23

This is fun!
Can you guess which
shape this was?

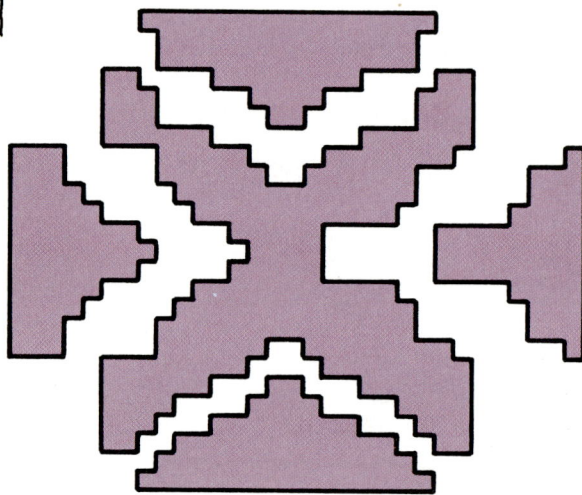

That was easy. Try this one.

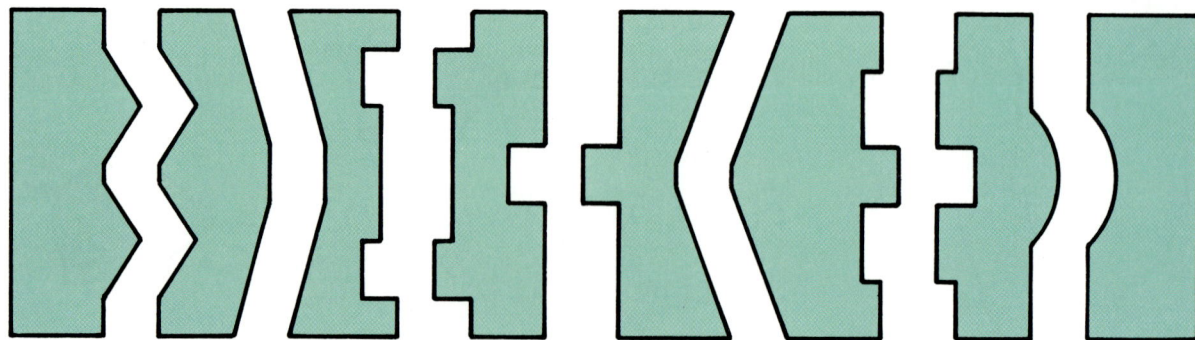

▶ Ask a grown-up which shapes these were.

The first shape was a _____.

The second shape was a _____.

Now try some more. Copy the shapes and cut along the dotted lines. You can ask a grown-up which shapes they were.
Take care with the scissors!

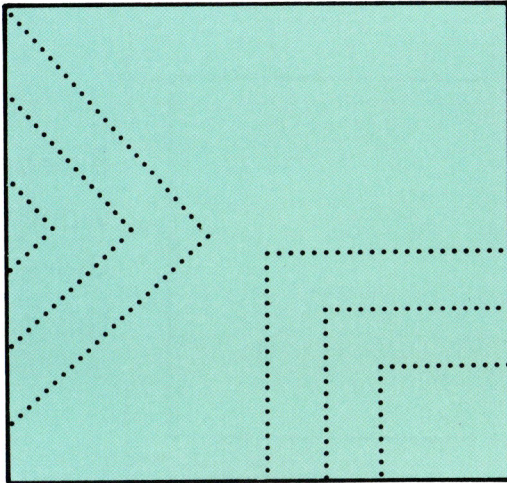

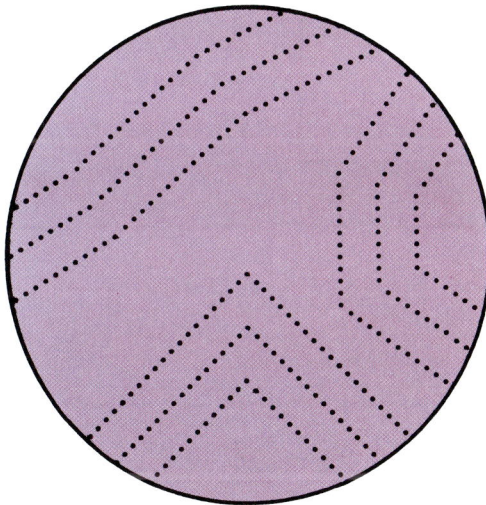

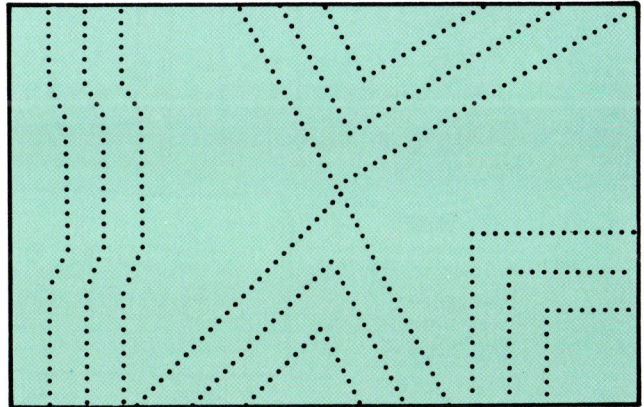

You can do the same thing from magazine pictures. Make sure everyone has read the magazine first, though!

13 Fair shares

Draw lines to show where to cut these cakes.

6 people want to share this one.

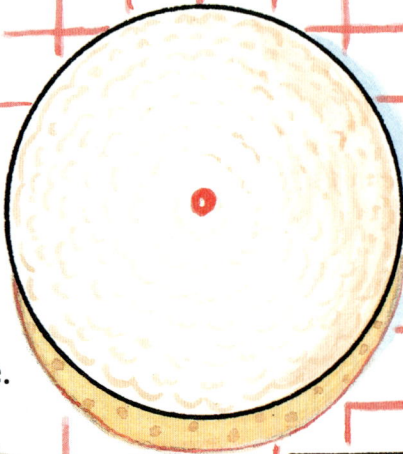

8 people want to share this one.

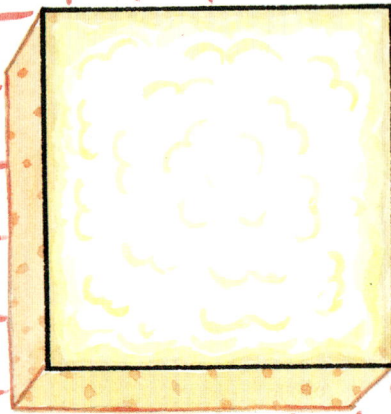

4 people want to share this one.

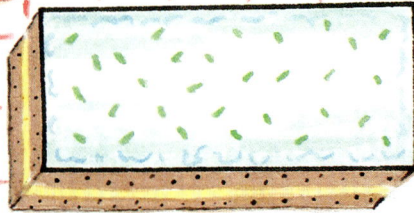

Share these sweets equally between . . .

. . . **3** people _____ sweets each.

. . . **4** people _____ sweets each.

. . . **6** people _____ sweets each.

. . . **8** people _____ sweets each.

. . . **12** people _____ sweets each.

▶ Put the correct number on each toy mouse.

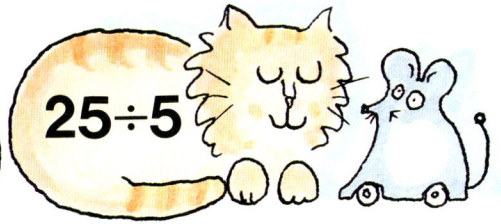

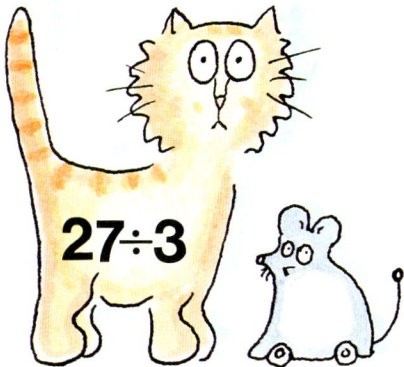

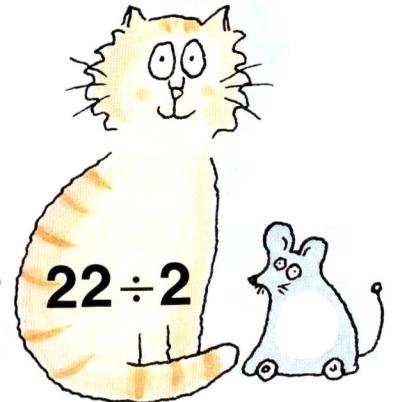

$16 \div 4$

$15 \div 3$

$25 \div 5$

$27 \div 3$

$32 \div 4$

$22 \div 2$

▶ Draw lines to show which bones the dogs can eat.

$35 \div 7$

$16 \div 2$

$20 \div 4$

$16 \div 4$

$8 \div 1$

$24 \div 6$

$24 \div 4$

$30 \div 10$

8

5

4

$40 \div 5$

6

3

$20 \div 5$

$15 \div 3$

$18 \div 3$

$12 \div 4$

I have chosen a shape. Follow the rules below to guess which one it is.

It is neither blue nor yellow.

It is not small.

It does not have straight sides.

It is a _____, _____, _____.

Now draw and colour the shapes covered by clouds.

Finish

Remember:

They can be either

▲ ■ ●

triangles   squares   circles

LARGE or small

red , blue or yellow

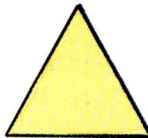

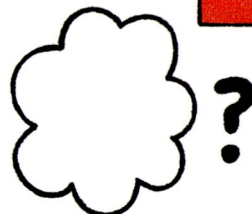

Colour the clowns

▶ Use red, blue and yellow to
make each clown different.

A

B

C

D

E

F

▶ Fill in the colour chart
to show what you did.

Clown	Hat	Flower	Bow
A			
B			
C			
D			
E			
F			

15 Calculator counting

You can use your calculator as a counting machine.

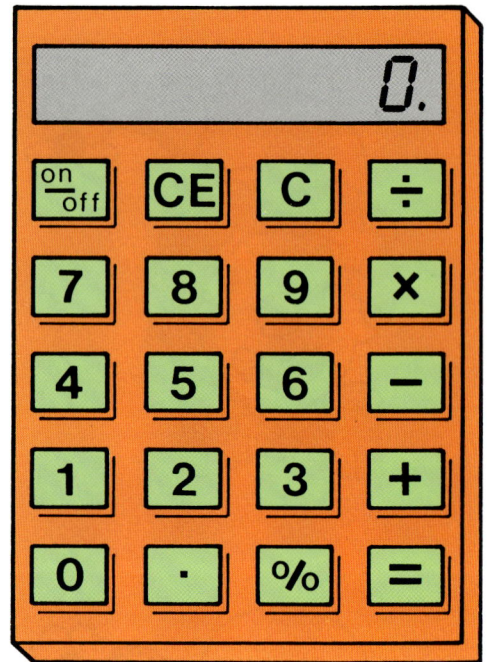

`0.`

on/off	CE	C	÷
7	8	9	×
4	5	6	−
1	2	3	+
0	·	%	=

Mary keyed in

[0] [+] [1] [=] [=] [=] [=] [=]

The display showed

`1.` then `2.` then `3.` then `4.` then `5.`

▶ Try this on your calculator.

▶ Key in the following and write down what the display shows each time you press [=]

[0] [+] [2] [=] [=] [=] [=] [=] [=] [=] [=] [=] [=]

Display shows: ___ ___ ___ ___ ___ ___ ___ ___ ___ ___

[3] [0] [+] [5] [=] [=] [=] [=] [=] [=] [=] [=] [=] [=]

Display shows: ___ ___ ___ ___ ___ ___ ___ ___ ___ ___

Make your calculator...

... Count in 2s from 8 to 28

8 __ __ __ __ __ __ __ __ __ **28**

... Count in 5s from 0 to 50

0 __ __ __ __ __ __ __ __ __ **50**

... Count in 10s from 100 to 200

100 __ __ __ __ __ __ __ __ __ **200**

... Count in 10s from 35 to 125

35 __ __ __ __ __ __ __ **125**

You can also use your calculator to count backwards.

`1` `0` `−` `1` `=` `=` `=` `=` `=` `=` `=` `=` `=`

▶ Try this on your calculator and write down what the display shows each time you press `=`

10 __ __ __ __ __ __ __

▶ Now make your calculator

... Count backwards in 2s from 24 to 0.

24 __ __ __ __ __ __ __ __ __ __ __ __

... Count backwards in 5s from 50 to 0.

50 __ __ __ __ __ __ __ __ __ __

... Count backwards in 10s from 500 to 390.

500 __ __ __ __ __ __ __ __ __ __ __

... Count backwards in 100s from 999 to 99.

999 __ __ __ __ __ __ __ __ __

Ruth, Leon, Tom and Mary were measuring the length of a nail. They only had broken pieces of rulers to use.

▶ Look at how they used their rulers.

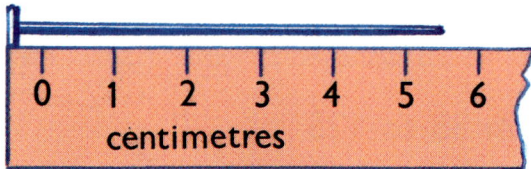

Ruth

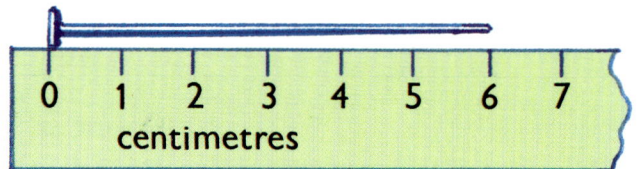

Leon

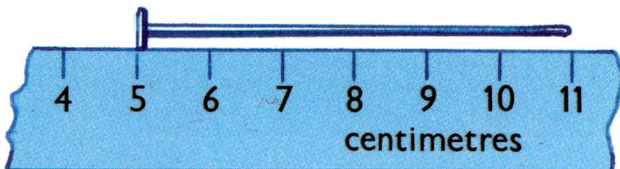

Tom

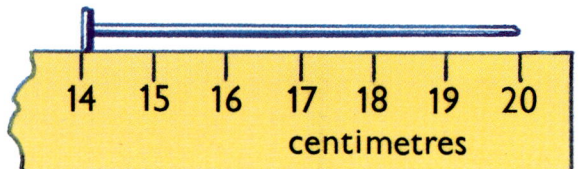

Mary

1 How long was the nail?

_____ cm

2 Three of the children gave the correct answer.
Who do you think gave the wrong answer?

_____

3 Why do you think this child got it wrong?

_____

_____

► Use a ruler to measure these objects.

_____ cm long

_____ cm tall

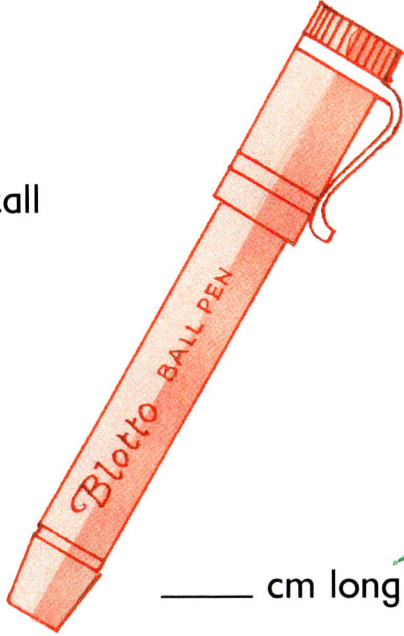

_____ cm long

_____ cm tall

_____ cm long

_____ cm high

_____ cm long

Watch and listen to the way some people count out your change on to your hand.

You have 50p.

18p

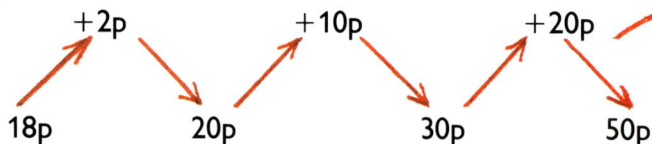

+2p   +10p   +20p

18p   20p   30p   50p

32p change.

You have 50p.

22p

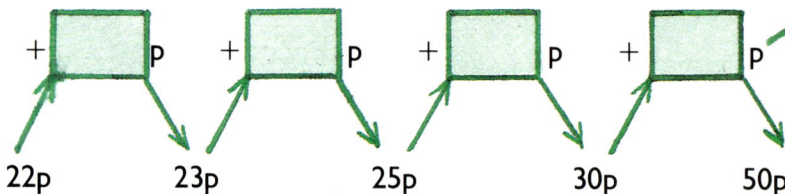

+ □ p   + □ p   + □ p   + □ p

22p   23p   25p   30p   50p

___ p change.

You have £1.

85p

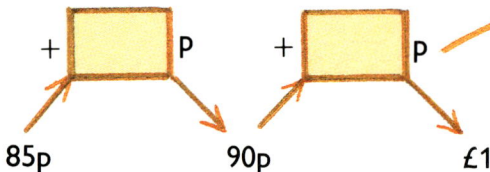

+ □ p   + □ p

85p   90p   £1

___ p change.

You have £5.

£3.38

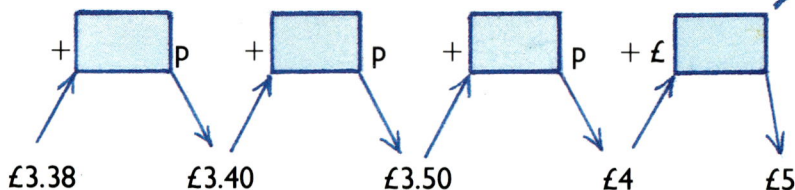

+ □ p   + □ p   + □ p   + £ □

£3.38   £3.40   £3.50   £4   £5

£ ___ change.

Alan, May, Joe and Ian had £5 to spend. Show how they checked their change.

I chose a set of felt-tipped pens which cost £1.25.

I chose a cuddly toy which cost £3.85.

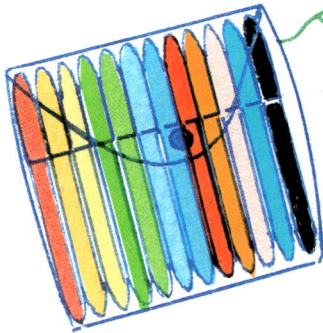

£1.25
+ 5p
£1.30
+ 20p
£1.50
+ 50p
£2.00
+ £1
£3.00
+ £1
£4.00
+ £1

The change is

_____

£3.85
+ ◯
▭
+ ◯
▭
+ ◯

The change is

_____

£5

The change is

_____

The change is

_____

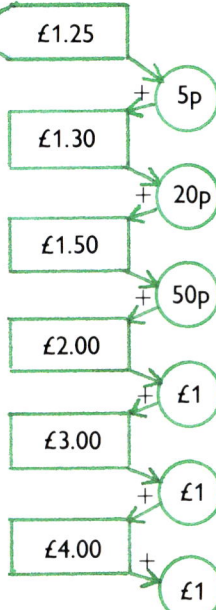

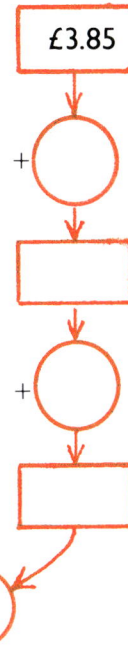

+ ◯
▭
+ ◯
▭
+ ◯
£4.38

+ ◯
◯
▭
+ ◯
▭
+ ◯
▭
+ ◯
£2.85

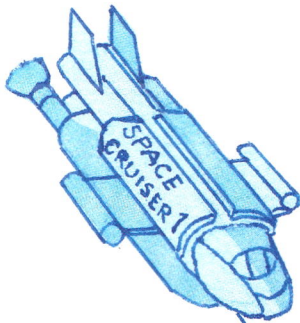

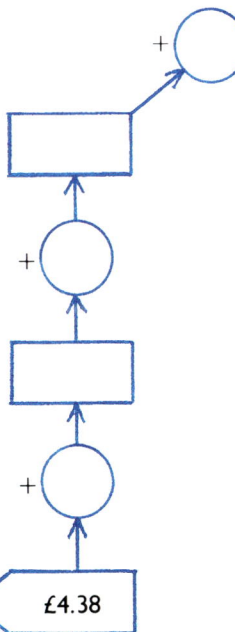

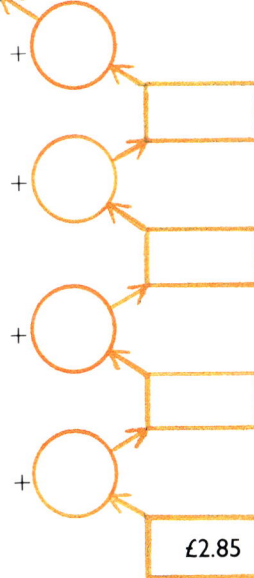

I chose a transformer toy which cost £4.38.

I chose a board game which cost £2.85.

Draw the other half of these pictures.
Holding a mirror along the dotted line will help.

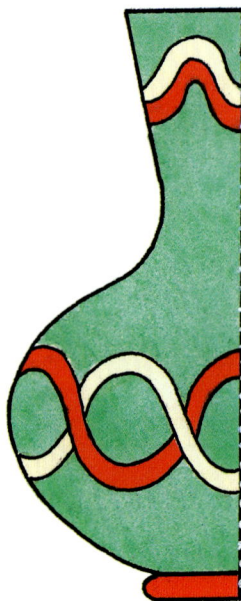

Make a mask

Draw the other half and cut out the mask. Stick this on to strong paper or card. You can make other masks, too!

You can play this game
with two or more players.

Here are the rules.

1. Take turns at joining one
   dot to the next with a line

   ——— or | but not ＼

2. You are trying to complete a box
   by joining up the fourth side.

3. If you complete a box, the score in that
   box is yours and you have another go.

| −3 | 11 | 6 |
| 14 | −8 | 9 |

→

| −3 | 11 | 6 |
| 14 | −8 | 9 |

I win this box
so I score 11.

4. Keep a note of your score as you play.

5. Play continues until all the boxes have been completed.

6. The player with the highest total score wins.

Any "minus" scores must
be subtracted!

Here are some grids to play boxing clever.

Game 1

10	30	45	60
50	15	5	40
20	55	35	20
10	25	5	15

Game 2

80	−10	40	−20
25	100	20	−40
−20	30	−15	60
50	−25	10	−30

Game 3

19	−6	17	24
−11	14	23	−15
28	−17	22	−8
21	−9	18	−13

Game 4

43	−15	65	−4
−21	33	14	−20
39	17	75	27
−26	51	−16	35

Try making up your own boxing clever grids.

You can make them as easy or as difficult as you like!

Answers

To Parents:

We have not provided *all* the answers here. We suggest that items to be drawn on clocks, snakes, etc., should be checked by you. In the case of activities where calculations are performed by your child, it would be good practice to get him/her to use a calculator to check the answers.

Unit No.	Answers
1	p. 3 Cuckoo clock – 2 o'clock; Sun-burst – 3.15; Wall clock – ten-thirty; Digital – quarter past 8; Alarm – half-past seven; Grandfather clock – six o'clock; Mantlepiece clock – quarter to 11.
2	p. 5 Child should spot that first four answers are the same . . . 15. 24 . . . −9 . . . 15 . . . −9 . . . 6 } Child may require clues before spotting these two 12 . . . +3 . . . 15 . . . +3 . . . 18 } patterns.
3	p. 7 Cylinder – 2 circles, 1 rectangle; Cuboid – 2 squares, 4 rectangles; Triangular prism – 2 triangles, 3 rectangles; Cube – 6 squares.
6	p. 12 52 31 121 110 19 102 166 304
7	p. 14 Crisps 32; Eggs 25 p. 15 Salt and vinegar crisps 33; Cheese and onion 24; 57 packets altogether. Brown eggs 44; white eggs 35; 79 eggs altogether.
8	p. 16 Numbers with both O and X are: 6, 12, 18, 24, 30, 36 . . . all multiples of 6. p. 17 Top: 18, 6, 30, 9, 10, 15, 14.
9	p. 19 **1** 31p; **2** 18p; **3** 58p; **4** 35p; **5** £1.15.
10	p. 21 **1** 7; **2** Dairy toffee; **3** Fudge; **4** 59.
11	pp. 22-23 **1** 8p; **2** 16p; **3** 19p; **4** 8p; **5** 15p; **6** 32p.
13	p. 26 8, 6, 4, 3, 2. p. 27 4, 5, 5, 9, 8, 11.
14	p. 28 Red, large, circle. 'Clouds' – small, yellow, triangle; small, blue, circle; large, red, triangle.
15	p. 30 2, 4, 6, 8, 10, 12, 14, 16, 18, 20. 35, 40, 45, 50, 55, 60, 65, 70, 75, 80. p. 31 10, 12, 14, 16, 18, 20, 22, 24, 26. 5, 10, 15, 20, 25, 30, 35, 40, 45. 110, 120, 130, 140, 150, 160, 170, 180, 190. 45, 55, 65, 75, 85, 95, 105, 115. 9, 8, 7, 6, 5, 4, 3, 2. 22, 20, 18, 16, 14, 12, 10, 8, 6, 4, 2, 0. 45, 40, 35, 30, 25, 20, 15, 10, 5, 0. 490, 480, 470, 460, 450, 440, 430, 420, 410, 400, 390. 899, 799, 699, 599, 499, 399, 299, 199, 99.
16	p. 32 **1** 6 cm; **2** Ruth; **3** Child should notice that Ruth has not started at zero, that is, at the end of the ruler rather than with a graduation or measuring mark. p. 33 Snake 11 cm; Shampoo 8 cm; Ballpen 9 cm; Tree 14 cm; Leaf 13 cm; Hat 5 cm; Caterpillar 10 cm.
17	p. 34 Ball 28p; Kite 15p; Yacht £1.62. p. 35 Felt-tips £3.75; Cuddly toy £1.15; Transformer 62p; Games £2.15.